Presented To:

From:

Date:

be the gift

Let Your Brokenness Be Turned into Abundance

ANN VOSKAMP

ZONDERVAN

Be the Gift

Copyright © 2017 by Ann Morton Voskamp

This title is also available as a Zondervan ebook.

Requests for information should be addressed to:
Zondervan, 3900 Sparks Dr. SE, Grand Rapids, Michigan 49546

Unless otherwise noted, Scripture quotations are taken from the Holy Bible, New International Version®, NIV®. Copyright © 1973, 1978, 1984, 2011 by Biblica, Inc.® Used by permission of Zondervan. All rights reserved worldwide. www.Zondervan.com. The "NIV" and "New International Version" are trademarks registered in the United States Patent and Trademark Office by Biblica, Inc.®

Scripture quotations marked ESV are taken from the ESV® Bible (The Holy Bible, English Standard Version®). Copyright © 2001 by Crossway, a publishing ministry of Good News Publishers. Used by permission. All rights reserved.

Scripture quotations marked HCSB are taken from the Holman Christian Standard Bible®. Copyright © 1999, 2000, 2002, 2003, 2009 by Holman Bible Publishers. Used by permission. HCSB® is a federally registered trademark of Holman Bible Publishers.

Scripture quotations marked MSG are taken from *The Message*. Copyright © by Eugene H. Peterson 1993, 1994, 1995, 1996, 2000, 2001, 2002. Used by permission of Tyndale House Publishers, Inc.

Scripture quotations marked NET are taken from the NET Bible®. Copyright © 1996–2006 by Biblical Studies Press, L.L.C. http://netbible.com. All rights reserved.

Scripture quotations marked NLT are taken from the *Holy Bible*, New Living Translation. © 1996, 2004, 2007, 2013 by Tyndale House Foundation. Used by permission of Tyndale House Publishers, Inc., Carol Stream, Illinois 60188. All rights reserved.

Any Internet addresses (websites, blogs, etc.) and telephone numbers in this book are offered as a resource. They are not intended in any way to be or imply an endorsement by Zondervan, nor does Zondervan vouch for the content of these sites and numbers for the life of this book.

ISBN 978-0-3100-8938-4

Published in association with William K. Jensen Literary Agency, 119 Bampton Court, Eugene, Oregon 97404.

Interior design: Lori Lynch

Printed in China
17 18 19 20 21   DSC   10 9 8 7 6 5 4 3 2 1

To Hope,

our first daughter—

your brave heart is always a gift to behold, to hold, to cherish.

You live your name like a gift everywhere you go.

Introduction

*S*ometimes in the stillness you can hear it, the sound of a million quiet-beating hearts.

We're all looking for it, searching desperately for the secret to abundance. *Will this bring what I'm seeking?* You can almost hear the asking echoing in every brave beat.

There's an answer we've got to find, if we're ever to find what we're seeking: *How in all this world do you live with your one broken heart?*

We've got to know the answer before we can hope to find what we're seeking. Because this world is beautiful—but this world is *broken.* And the suffering is all around us . . . in us.

And yet, for those who believe, this can be the very birthplace of healing beauty.

Though your heart will be broken, this is where light will

get in, where love will get in. And though you may know great suffering, that's right where the greatest love can embrace you.

Knowing this, *living this*, could change everything.

We can find gratitude in all things, learn to count the gifts and awaken to the fact that all is grace in our one brutal and beautiful life. And yet there can come a heart-wrenching struggle and the sudden question of what to do with your brokenness.

If you're truly paying attention to all God brings, you can't help but acknowledge that He has allowed—even brought us— brokenness and suffering. And even if we can find gratitude for it, still we must discover how to move forward *in it*.

This dare to be the gift is a call to let your brokenness be turned into abundance. A call to act and live out the brave and the bold beauty of *The Broken Way*. Even in the depths of our own brokenness—actually, *because* of the depths of our own brokenness—God can use each of us to be a gift to another broken heart. He makes us enough, makes our brokenness into abundance, to give to the brokenhearted. And in healing, we find healing.

Our every act can be an act of hope, of choosing to be the

gift in a broken world, to be the love making a broken world know more of its belovedness.

The thrilling secret beyond all suffering is that even—*especially*—in that place of suffering, we can become God's gifts to others, and we can taste the actual goodness of His abundance.

Maybe the only abundant way forward—is always to give ourselves forward? To be the broken and brave who know that when the stakes are the highest, kindness matters the most. To believe that the bad brokenness of the world is met by the good brokenness of Christ's humble sacrifice for us.

Even the smallest seeds of kindness can begin to break the worst kind of brokenness.

Yes, it's true—our hearts may be busted and bruised . . . but I just keep repeating the healing secret of what to do with your one broken heart: *give it away, because this is how you begin to heal.* Because there is no deep healing in our hearts until we are part of deep healing in the world. Because the best way to love in a brokenhearted world is to feel along for the brokenness in things, and to give our own hearts to that brokenness *and make a kind of wholeness.*

We keep healing as we keep being healers. In being the gift of healing for someone's brokenness, we receive a gift of healing for our own brokenness.

We could listen for the pain in the world today and pour love into it. Listen for the ache today and give your heart today, because the broken of the world need His touch. This might be a step toward the healing we are all desperately needing. Maybe God's purposes come not so much through power but through the compassion of God's people. This compassion that literally means co-suffering. Co-suffering with the suffering is how Jesus chose to literally transform the suffering.

What if we listened well to each other's broken hearts, to each other's suffering? What if we could be compassionate with each other, *co-suffer* with each other—so that we could be part of *the healing of each other*?

Our call is to be compassionate, to be a community, a communion, of broken bread and poured-out wine, to live cruciform, formed like a cross. Our call is to take the form of reaching hands, open ears, listening hearts because our God is with us and we're called into communion with Him and with each other. Because our compassionate God is all-powerful and we cannot help but be compassionate with each other because this is the way of the most powerful.

If you lean in close, you can hear it, the faint heartbeat of a strong hope, of people coming together to give grace to each other, to *be the gift* to each other, through the brokenness of everything being re-membered . . . everything being put back together.

So here's to being the gift, to listening to others and seeing the opportunities to be God's gifts every day of the year. Here's to the thanksgiving that becomes *thanks-living* in our everyday lives.

Here's to the beginning of a new journey, of chronicling the way to truly living in communion, and opening ourselves up in every season to givenness—because of our our brokenness . . . because of our living like the bread of communion, broken and given—a gift—into an abundant communion.

May this be to you a starting place to finally discover what it means to be a GIFT—to Give It Forward Today—and find the truly abundant life.

All is grace—all is a gift.

Ann Voskamp

from a grateful evening on the farm

We lost the day in love. You can be glued to a screen or glued to your schedule or glued to your stuff—and maybe that's just a bit of lost living. You can be a slave to getting ahead, a slave to the clock, a slave to convenience, a slave to some ill-advised American dream—and maybe that's a lot of lost living.

Maybe even in a bit of brokenness, grace moves in you to get up and give to people you love and people you're learning to love, to go to the park and laugh with your kids or any kids, to give an elderly woman a hand and a listening ear and the gift of presence—that's large living.

The greatest living always happens through the givenness.

I don't even know who has the audacious idea to go up to the dollar store and leave dollars up and down every aisle, but our kids watch unsuspecting kids wander in. Smiles break up every aisle.

And maybe a bit of the world's brokenness breaks by this good brokenness.

This boy in a ball cap stops at the counter and picks up a lollipop we've taped a note to: "Here's a dollar. Pick any color. We're Giving It Forward Today. #betheGIFT." His face explodes in this smile, and bits of joy lodge in the brokenness of me and I feel a bit remade.

Smiling at anyone is to awe at the face of God.

And "the beauty of the world is Christ's tender smile coming to us through matter" (Simone Weil). There's a clerk grinning at the till. The guy stocking shelves is chuckling. There are people Giving It Forward Today, and don't think that every gift of grace, every act of kindness, isn't a quake in a heart that moves another heart to give, that moves another heart to give, that grows into an avalanche of grace.

Don't say this isn't what a brokenhearted world desperately needs; don't say it isn't how to change a broken world.

What if the truth really is that every tremor of kindness here erupts in a miracle elsewhere in the world?

I can feel it like the slightest sense of a suturing along raw and ragged scar lines. Maybe our suffering and brokenness begin a kind of healing when we enter into the suffering and brokenness of the world, right through the brokenness and givenness of Christ.

And these acts of kindness, gifts of grace, they start a cascade of grace to fill a multitude of canyons in a hurting world. Maybe there's no such thing as a small act of giving. Every small gift of grace creates a love quake that has no logical end. It will go to the ends of the earth and change the world, and then it will break through time and run on into eternity.

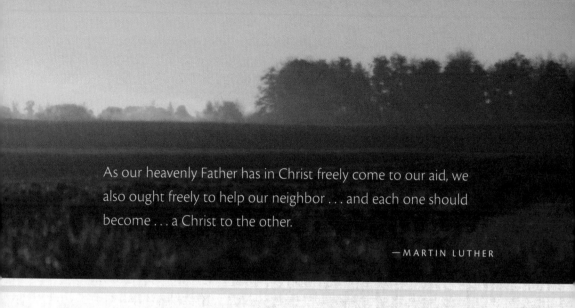

As our heavenly Father has in Christ freely come to our aid, we also ought freely to help our neighbor . . . and each one should become . . . a Christ to the other.

—MARTIN LUTHER

I would read later that those who perform five acts of giving over six weeks are happier than those who don't, that when you give, you get reduced stress hormone levels, lowered blood pressure, and increased endorphins, and that acts of kindness reduce anxiety and strengthen the immune system. Five random acts of kindness in a week can increase happiness for up to three months later. "He gives by cartloads to those who give by bushels," wrote Spurgeon, and I'd think of that tin bucket with its 25,550 kernels of wheat.

Maybe if all you have to give are handfuls, He might make a broken heart full?

The happiness of givenness is a balm that works its healing even days and weeks later, and givenness does not define or prove our value *but lets us feel the defining value of love*. Givenness changes our body because we become part of His Body. And we are even fed communion through our own brokenness. Maybe even in any of our misguided motives of givenness, even then, we are guided back to communion to reap the benefits of love.

"And the one who gives a drink of water will receive water" (Proverbs 11:25 HCSB).

There's this elixir in the veins, and giving is always the greatest, the most beautiful of all, because maybe giving is the shape of what love is—cruciform. Love gives.

Love must give to the beautiful people in the backstreets of wherever our feet land, beautiful people living near us and sitting across from us and streaming by us, and no matter what anyone's saying, everyone's just asking if they can be loved.

Love gives and every smile says, *Yes, you are loved.*

"Give away your life; you'll find life given back, but not merely given back— given back with bonus and blessing. Giving, not getting, is the way."

—LUKE 6:38 MSG

After I give a box of chocolates to the nurses up on the pediatric floor, I turn to the Farmer and say it slowly to him, "For an introvert feeling messy and broken and battling the edge of depression, it takes ridiculous stores of courage to keep reaching out, to break out of your comfort zone and give like this."

But look at what Christ did!

Maybe—maybe there's a Comforter who holds us gently in our brokenness . . . which is very different from a comfort zone that's a death trap to break us.

And the art of really living may just involve figuring out that difference.

When we walk in the back door from Sunday service, from the breaking of bread and thick intimacy of exchange, there's this black pen lying on the table.

I pick up the pen and turn my wrist over. How many years had I cut that paling wrist, wearing my brokenness on the outside? I pick up the pen, and on a whim—on a conviction, kind of ridiculously desperate to remember the radical symbolism, to remember the union, the communion—I write it on my wrist, let it bleed like a vow right there into the thin white skin: one little black cross.

I am busted and His, and He is broken and given and mine.

I trace that one black cross: *Can you dare to break yourself into a kind of communion, a kind of union? Can you let the way be made for broken places to re-member?*

It's like this is one wild dare to live cruciform, to let life become shaped like a cross. This could be a dare to let life be shaped like union.

It's a dare to be married to mysteries so Christ has hands again in this world—and specifically mine.

ALL IS SACRED IN THE GIVENNESS—THE
GIVENNESS OF GOD THROUGH EVERYTHING,
THE SURRENDER OF EVERYTHING TO HIM.

Just take the first step. And then the next step. Courage is reaching out and taking just a bit of that iron-nail grace.

A book sits in a pond of light on the edge of the dresser. In the kitchen, a crumbling handful of yesterday's cookies sits on a plate. When I wander out to the red mailbox at the end of our lane, I leave a book and brown paper bag of cookies for the mail carrier.

On the way in, I will myself to pick a bunch of zinnias and glads from the weedy, tangled patch masquerading as a garden. I say their name out loud as I pick—"glads, glads, glads." *Remind me. Rewire me.* That cross on my wrist begs like a prayer:

Become cruciform.

Like a cross. Transform.

If it is True that to become cruciform, to let your life become shaped like a cross, is to become more fully human—and most fully like Christ—then this is the work most urgent, most needed.

There's a cross that is your backbone, and all you have to do is reach out your arms.

The way to find the light in the dark is to make your hand reach out—reach out in thanks, reach out in giving. And maybe your hand has to reach out so your heart keeps beating—so someone else keeps breathing. Maybe this can be a way to keep breaking the bread and reaching out to pass it down, right through brokenness.

How can I not keep reaching out while I'm still alive?

THE WAY TO BREAK TIME'S HOLD ON ME IS
TO BE BROKEN AND GIVEN WITH MY TIME.

There are only so many full orbits around the sun, and who makes time to lie in bed and listen to rain thrumming on roofs or to take someone for strawberry ice cream sundaes and linger down at the bridge, the river running underneath like the present running through your hands? And there are glads to be picked from the earth and there is time yet to live in the givenness of everything.

Your time is limited—so don't limit your life by wanting someone else's.

Sometimes I stand in the living room after they're all in bed and listen to that clock tick slowly. Sometimes the ticking of the clock is like Morse code, tapping it out again and again:

You have only one decision every day: how will you use your time?

Sometimes the best use of your time is to stand and listen to a clock. We're all terminal—and we all just want a number. *What size is this bucket of time? How many days do I actually get?*

The hands of the clock are bound by the decisions of our hands. And He has made our hands free to be His.

"Unless a grain of wheat falls into the earth and dies, it remains alone; but if it dies, it bears much fruit" (John 12:24 ESV).

Die to self—and have twice as much life.

There's a way to multiply your life. You let every kernel die.

The shape of multiplied time looks like a cross. Cruciform. Broken and given, reaching right out.

There's enough time yet for picking glads and filling Mason jar vases of blooms for sidelined, forgotten people. There's time for lingering over cups of coffee and listening to the pouring out of someone's cracked heart, time for long phone calls and shared pie and going the extra mile. And there's time to be broken and given into all the world's brokenness, because this is how to break time's hold.

I grab that tin bucket the Farmer left on the top step at the back door. I pour every single one of the 25,550 wheat kernels out of that dusty Mason jar that's been sitting up there on the windowsill since the beginning of the year, looking like a time capsule. Like a dare to break time.

I fill it with water and glads and schlepp a bunch of those jar vases over to the nursing home. The kids and I leave them in the doorways of the residents' rooms, and there's no missing the beauty of what these have held and what they're containers for now—or how entire wings of the nursing home light up in these thousand-watt smiles. On hard days of wrestling with time and pieces of your broken past, turns out you can always find a way to reach out your hand and just turn the light on.

Maybe the only abundant way forward is always to give forward.

It's all like a slow match in me that could start an explosion. Could there be a better way to spend time than to break through the anxiety that keeps a life bound and small? What if it detonated in my own heart: reach out your one weak arm and let your own brokenness start to mend?

Can I trust that He's enough in me to make me enough? This is all part of the figuring, the finding of the way.

Maybe because the clock was ticking loud while I filled those Mason jars, maybe that's what made me think of how I had wanted to spend my fortieth birthday, giving it forward, being a gift of His grace. Or maybe it was the filling of the Mason jars. Maybe because it *was* my birthday and I could choose what I wanted, and what I wanted was to not waste any more of time that keeps running through my fingers like water. Maybe because I'd thought of what Elizabeth with her terminal cancer had told me.

Hearts are broken in ten thousand ways,
for this is a heart-breaking world; and Christ
is good at healing all manner of heart-breaks.

—CHARLES SPURGEON

I'd looked right into the watery hope of her eyes when she said that whenever she met with her doctor in that sterile white room, what she wanted most was a number. What all terminal patients really want is a number.

"How long have I got, Doc?"

Elizabeth had said it directly, like she wanted to lodge it squarely into me. "The real wrestling in living and in dying is always a wrestle for a number."

My Elizabeth was dying, and she still hadn't any idea how much time she actually had to live. Maybe knowing you're dying changes everything—*while actually changing nothing*. Because we all know it every single day, whether we have a diagnosis or not:

We all get one container of time—but no one gets to know what size that container is.

Who doesn't know what it's like to smile thinly and say you're fine when you're not, when you're almost faint with pain? There isn't one of us not bearing the wounds from our own bloody battles.

There isn't one of us who isn't cut right from the beginning.

All of us get pushed from safe wombs out into this holy mess. All of us need someone to catch us and hold us right from the beginning, and for one sacred moment, every single one of us is cupped. And then they cut that one thick umbilical cord. You can spend a lifetime feeling pushed out, cut off, abandoned— inexplicably alone.

What in God's holy name do you do when it feels like you're broken and cut up, and love has failed, and you've failed, and you feel like Somebody's love has failed you?

Not one thing in your life is more important than figuring out how to live in the face of unspoken pain.

It's a strange thing to find out your heart can explode with love and suffering and find out they're kin in ways we don't care to admit. *I don't know the way to put all these broken pieces back into place. Maybe that's the point?*

Maybe this broken way is making something new. *He is making all things new.*

Jesus died crying.

Jesus died of a broken heart. Those words were still warm on His cracked lips: "My God, my God, why have you forsaken me?" (Matthew 27:46). The movement of a life of faith is always toward answering that singular question.

I can see that question hanging over our farm table, up in the gable, from that framed canvas of a thousand little broken squares of color. In the semiabstract painting, there's no tidy pattern, just light and dark bleeding into this subtle suggestion of Jesus hanging on the cross. He's hoarse with the begging, for Himself, for us: "God, why have You

abandoned Me?" And He surfaces in the patches of color, the broken brushstrokes, the silhouette of Him visible in the chaos—Christ entering all this chaos.

There is the truth: Blessed—lucky—are those who cry. Blessed are those who are sad, who mourn, who feel the loss of what they love—because they will be held by the One who loves them. There is a strange and aching happiness only the hurting know—for they shall be held.

I believed this then and believe it now and I'd say I know it to be true—but there is more than believing—there is living what you believe.

Do I really?

Sometimes I stand in the living room after they're all in bed and listen to that clock tick slowly. Sometimes the ticking of the clock is like Morse code, tapping it out again and again:

You have only one decision every day: how will you use your time?

Sometimes the best use of your time is to stand and listen to a clock. We're all terminal—and we all just want a number. *What size is this bucket of time? How many days do I actually get?*

Back when the calendar flung itself into a new year, our youngest one with the sprinkle of freckles across her nose asked me how many days a person gets to live, and I didn't know what to say. I'd told her that maybe, maybe her number was 25,550?

How do you tell a child that time is a vapor and that even if you reach your hand out, it will run through like water and fall like dew and soon will all be gone?

Shalom had laughed like a hoot owl, rolled across the white quilt of my bed. "You're making it up now, Mama."

"I ain't." I yanked one of her curled bare toes. She felt like tangle-headed adventures and sticky buns on Saturday mornings and the creek rising in the back woods and unbridled hope—an unfurling. She felt like time embraced.

"Why would your crazy old mama make up a number like that?"

Her freckles had crinkled. "She would!"

"Well, *if* you get seventy years—*if*—then from the day you're born till you fly away Home, you'd get 25,550 days. That's your number, girl—maybe."

God, give us whole buckets of time. And "the man who would know God must give time to Him" (A. W. Tozer). It's like the cross penned into skin is silently pleading.

Shalom sat up on the bed, like she'd seen something. Like she needed to understand it.

She pulls her knees up to her chin. "What's a number like that look like?"

"It looks like . . ."

Time looks like light caught in the limbs of willing trees, I think, like laugh lines bracketing a thousand brave smiles, like a steady current of wrinkled sheets and slow dawns, of steam rising off bowls, of opening and closing back doors and the click of thousands of last lights out. Time is always a stream of God's "unbounded Now," C. S. Lewis wrote.

It looks like a river of Nows. Unbounded. Broken free.

Is there any word more
powerful than *giving*?
Thanksgiving.
Forgiving.
Care-giving.
Life-giving.
Everything that matters in living
comes down to giving.

"To get a glass jar."

She slides off the bed, eyes watching mine. She finds an old blue Mason jar with wavy, bubbled glass and hands it to me. It's smooth and sure in my palm. I turn it over. A jar in my hands. A cross written over the scars on my wrist. Hauling out the large bag of wheat used to make bread, I stand in front of the pantry and measure out four cups of kernels.

We pour them, careful not to drop the jar.

"There's your 25,550 days," I say.

Our girl rolls the jar between her hands. *There's your life,* I think. *How will you live with your one broken heart?* The kernels of wheat rain against the glass. Take your one container of time and believe it contains exactly the time you need for a meaningful life.

She holds the jar up to the light, liquefying it into gold. "All we are . . . are these grain days."

These grain days. These grace days.

And that's all I keep coming back to: *"Unless a grain of wheat falls into the earth and dies, it remains alone; but if it dies, it bears much fruit"* (John 12:24 ESV).

The same hand that unwraps the firmaments of winging stars wraps liniments around the wounded heart; the One whose breath births galaxies into being births healing into the hearts of the broken.

All of us in a heart-breaking world, we are the fellowship of the broken. Over all of us is the image of the wounded God, the God who breaks open and bleeds with us.

Only the wounds of God can heal our wounds. This is the truth, and I feel the rising of it: suffering is healed by suffering, wounds are healed by wounds.

It jars me, shatters my fears into the softness of Him: bad brokenness in the world is healed by His good brokenness of grace.

*Bad brokenness is broken
by good brokenness.*

Maybe the love gets in easier right where the heart's broke open.

Maybe you can live a full and beautiful life in spite of the great and terrible moments that will happen right inside of you. Actually—maybe you get to *become* more abundant *because* of those moments.

Maybe—I don't know how, but somehow?—maybe our hearts are made to be broken. Broken open. Broken free. Maybe the deepest wounds birth deepest wisdom.

We are made in the image of God. And wasn't God's heart made to be broken too? Wounds can be openings to the beauty in us. And our weaknesses can be a container for God's glory.

Hannah tasted salty tears of infertility. Elijah howled for God to take his life. David asked his soul a thousand times why it was so downcast. God does great things through the greatly wounded. God sees the broken as the best and He sees the best in the broken and He calls the wounded to be the world changers.

Our bad brokenness is made whole by His good brokenness.

When we know Christ, we always know how things are going to go—always for our good and always for His glory.

Somehow Love can lodge light into wounds.

The warming spring sun falls behind him standing at the kitchen window. All across the field to the east, the wheat waves like a brazen promise.

I'll take it. I'll take what the Farmer had once said to me like a daring covenant, not knowing yet what's to come: there is no growth without change, no change without surrender, no surrender without wound—no abundance without breaking. Wounds are what break open the soul to plant the seeds of a deeper growth.

My dad had told me this once. For a seed to come fully into its own, it must become wholly undone. The shell must break open, its insides must come out, and everything must change. If you didn't understand what life looks like, you might mistake it for complete destruction.

Brokenness can make abundance.

Where is the abundant life? And how in the world to find it?

"And he took bread, gave thanks and broke it, and gave it to them . . ."

I had first read it slowly, years ago—how in the original language "gave thanks" reads *eucharisteo*. The root word of *eucharisteo* is *charis*, meaning "grace." Jesus took the bread and saw it as grace and gave thanks.

There was more. *Eucharisteo*, thanksgiving, also holds the Greek word *chara*, meaning "joy." Joy. And that was what the quest for more has always been about—that which Augustine claimed, "Without exception . . . all try their hardest to reach the same goal, that is, joy."

Deep *chara* is found only at the table of the *euCHARisteo*—the table of thanksgiving.

I had sat there long . . . wondering . . . is it that simple? *Is the height of my* chara *joy dependent on the depths of my* eucharisteo *thanks?*

In Christ—no matter the way, the storm, the story—we always know the outcome. Our Savior—surrounds. Our future—secure. Our joy—certain.

So then as long as thanks was possible, then joy was always possible. The holy grail of joy was not in some exotic location or some emotional mountain peak experience. The joy wonder could be here, in the messy, piercing ache of now. The only place we need see before we die is this place of seeing God, *here and now*.

I'd whispered it out loud, let the tongue feel these sounds, the ear hear their truth.

Charis. Grace. *Eucharisteo.* Thanksgiving. *Chara.* Joy.

Why are we afraid of broken things? I can think of a thousand raw reasons. But touch the broken and the hungry and the hurting and the thirsty and the busted, and you touch a bit of Christ. *Why are we afraid of suffering?* What if the abundance of communion is only found in the brokenness of suffering— because suffering is where God lives? Suffering is where God gives the most healing intimacy.

What if . . . what if I made a habit of every day pressing my wounds into the wounds of Christ—could my brokenness be made into a healing abundance for the brokenness of the world? A kind of communion? Could all brokenness meet in the mystery of Christ's brokenness and givenness and become the miracle of abundance? Wouldn't that be good brokenness breaking bad brokenness?

The strength of the reality weakens the knees here a bit. A paradigm shift—more like an earthquake, like a foundation is breaking. Breaking open.

Is this way realest life—or is life really this way?

This feels like a dare that is choosing me. I don't know if I know how to do this. I don't know if I *want* to do this.

The sun pools. The floor lights, everything lights: there is no physical body of Christ here on earth but ours. We are now Christ's only earthly body—and if we aren't the ones broken and given, we are the ones who dis-member Christ's body. Unless we are the ones broken and given, we incapacitate Christ's body on earth.

Maybe—there is no breaking of bad brokenness unless His people become good brokenness. Living broken and given like bread.

The creation of the world seems to have been especially for this end, that the eternal Son of God might obtain a spouse towards whom he might fully exercise the infinite benevolence of his nature, and to whom he might, as it were, open and pour forth all that immense fountain of condescension, love, and grace that was in his heart.

—JONATHAN EDWARDS

Continuously make the ever-present Christ present. Continuously be part of the remembering of brokenness. This happens every Sunday. When you're a bloodied mess with that cursed chronic soul amnesia, it is good to remember your soul is dangerously emaciated for a reviving taste of His memory.

We ingest the broken. We become the broken. The wheat was crushed. Every kernel shattered for this bread. Every grape was crushed. The sweetness ran in the brokenness.

In shattered places, with broken people, we are most near the broken heart of Christ and find our whole selves through the mystery of death and resurrection, through the mystery of brokenness and abundance.

We are the body sustained by His brokenness, His givenness, sustained by this Last Supper that for centuries was called simply "the thanksgiving"—the *eucharistias*.

"I say to you, unless a grain of wheat falls into the earth and dies, it remains alone; but if it dies, it bears much fruit."

—JOHN 12:24 ESV

Death and resurrection. The paradox of it breaks into me afresh: unless we die, unless we surrender, unless we sacrifice, we remain alone. *Lonely.* But if we die, if we surrender, if we sacrifice, if we live given, that is when we experience the abundance, that is when we dance in communion. The life that yields the most— *yields* the most.

The fields to the south sing in the surrender of it: "But if you let it go, reckless in your love, you'll have it forever, real and eternal" (John 12:25 MSG).

I've got to let it go.

And the Farmer hands me the basket of communion bread. What do you do if you feel too wounded, too devastated to receive? Sometimes desperation drives you through devastation. I break off my piece of the loaf. *This is My body*—and the crushed kernels dissolve into me, become me. The wheat seed grew into a wheat stalk that ripened and was broken and came to my brokenness. If you didn't know how bread is made, you might think it looks like complete destruction.

Can you dare to break yourself into communion?

You can forget there's any light in living, in your soul. You can find it hard to remember.

Anxiety can come out of nowhere. Get busy, get distracted, and you can forget God. Forget God, and you lose your mind and your peace. Forget God, and all you remember is anxiety. Anxiety can give you God-Alzheimer's. Forget the face of God, and you forget your own name is Beloved.

Is anything you're doing here adding up to anything that matters? And in the end, is what you've chosen ultimately about Christ and His kingdom?

How can all the bad brokenness be broken with good brokenness? How do you live cruciform—and be broken and given like bread, broken and given into a kind of communion?

Who knows why God allows heartbreak, but the answer must be important enough because God allows His heart to break too.

I reach for the pen on my nightstand, the way I've

Ultimately it comes down to this, that the real cause of our trouble is failure to realize our union with Christ.

—MARTYN LLOYD-JONES

reached for ink to count a thousand ways He loves me, the way ink's been the cheapest of medicines. But now—can the ink be lived, branded onto the skin, how could it leave the page and lead a way through pain? The ink would start right there on my scarred wrist, right where part of me wanted to kind of die, and not in the saving way, and somehow there is good brokenness that grows out of every scar and wound we will ever suffer.

Our broken hearts always break His.

The art of giving is believing there is enough love in you because He is in you, that you are loved enough by Him, to be made enough love to give.

For God so loved that He gave . . . Is there any word more powerful than *giving*? *Thanksgiving. Forgiving. Care-giving. Life-giving.* Everything that matters in living comes down to giving.

"Giving is true having," is what Spurgeon said. The love of God always gives, always breaks itself and gives—*to give joy.* God seeks His own glory only because He vows that He is the God who gives—gives what we need most.

"What I'm interested in seeing you do is: sharing your food with the hungry, inviting the homeless poor into your homes, putting clothes on the shivering ill-clad, being available to your own families. Do this and the lights will turn on, and your lives will turn around at once. Your righteousness will pave your way. The GOD of glory will secure your passage. Then when you pray, GOD will answer. You'll call out for help and I'll say, 'Here I am'" (Isaiah 58:7–9 MSG).

Are the most painful tears the kind
no one can see, the kind where
your soul weeps alone?

What we break and give comes back to us as a bit of communion. *Koinonia*, a soul sharing, a givenness, a participation. The very moment of my *salvation* in Christ made my *union* with Christ an objective *fact*, but it's not until this moment of realization of *communion* with Christ that there's *experiential* joy.

This is a sort of communion.

When you walk into a diner across the street and tell the waitress you're paying for that family's dinner, it's a thing you don't forget, and it feels like an act of re-membering. The waitress laughs and you wink and leave before they're finished at the all-you-can-eat buffet. A diner and hungry people and the presence of Christ in you, reaching your unsure hand out, can taste like a sacrament.

Live eucharist. Practice communion. Taste *koinonia*. Feel abundant life. All I can think is this: *this is how you make the ever-present Christ fully present.* This is the beginning of becoming the gift. Allow Christ in you to give away the gift of Himself right through your brokenness. God gives God so we can be the givers. The gift-ers.

Do you hesitate, man, to go this way,

when this is the way that God came to you?

—AUGUSTINE

Being in pursuit of Him as He relentlessly pursues me in this growing intimacy had brought me sooner or later to this, this dare to live the communion of living the shape of the cross, living cruciform.

The boys gift the tennis court with a whole bunch of tennis balls. And I slip into the back door of the library, leave a few of my favorite books at the desk; then the whole lot of us circle over to the grocery store on Mitchell Street, put away grocery carts, grab a few bags of groceries, and drop them off at the food bank. Stick quarters into bubble gum machines at Walmart. Scope out the grocery store to buy a cart of groceries for someone. Tuck parking fees into envelopes, and slide them under windshield wipers for those in the hospital parking lot.

Time is made for dying in a thousand ways, so why be afraid of dying when a kind of dying could come all the time? Live every day like you're terminal. Because you are. Live every day like your soul's eternal. *Because it is.*

There is a time to be comforted . . . and a time to come and die into a greater kind of comfort. And like that song of givenness running under and through the atoms of the universe, the Farmer says the verses quietly: "If you spend yourselves in behalf of the hungry and satisfy the needs of the oppressed . . ." (Isaiah 58:10).

And I turn in the shade of the old maples lining the hospital parking lot and join him: ". . . then your light will rise in the darkness, and your night will become like the noonday."

The light feels warm. Dappled on faces. The Farmer only nods to me. There's not much to say when you feel a holy change beginning: our broken night could become like the noonday. Light could rise in all this darkness—in us, in the ache of unspoken broken, in all this busted world.

"THERE'S A WAY TO BREAK BROKENNESS.
AND WHAT IF YOU LET IT FULLY
COME . . . LET IT COME?"

Hand over your whole self. Your whole broken self. *Givenness.* Because this is far easier than pretending to be whole and not broken.

There is a strange sense of surrender happening, a surrender in all things. The heart has to be broken and plowed and re-sown if it's going to yield. The change must go deeper than the surface. This is only the beginning. There's a bucket of wheat at the back door—time—and there's enough given to you to satisfy your soul—everything you need. And if you want your life to yield, there has to be a yielding in the soul. There is a plowing that breaks your soul to grow you.

SPENDING YOURSELF IS HOW YOU PAY
ATTENTION TO JOY; SPENDING YOURSELF
IS HOW YOU *MULTIPLY JOY.*

Keeping ink on the nightstand can be a kind of curative, my intravenous needle to remember the *eucharisteo* every night and send a bit of the thanks into the blood. I am "called into the *koinonia* of His Son, Jesus Christ" (1 Corinthians 1:9, paraphrased). I know this. The *eucharisteo* precedes the miracle, and the miracle is always, always *koinonia*. But maybe I haven't been living it long enough yet?

How do you believe there is enough of you to live given—and be wanted?

The wheat in the fields needed this rain that's sheeting down like some upstairs plumbing let loose. The sky slides down the windowpane next to the bathroom mirror like something a bit busted.

I need these questions, need answers to fall, to grow something in me strong enough to withstand this broken life. If I want to truly Give It Forward Today, if I want to be the gift, don't I have to believe there's enough in me that's a gift to give forward? Maybe we believe in Jesus; we just don't always believe in Him *working in us.*

65

We in our brokenness believe in God—*and God believes in us through our brokenness*. Because we've asked Christ to take our brokenness and give us His righteousness.

Can I believe in God, in Jesus, in a way that I know Jesus believes in me—because I know that Christ Himself gave Himself for me, died for me, dwells deeply within me? Maybe it isn't enough to believe in Jesus—maybe I have to believe that Jesus believes enough in me to choose me—because He's made me, loves me, died for me, is in me. If Christ has chosen me, If He's the only One who has ever loved me to death—can He *not* believe in me? *Can I believe Jesus believes in me—because He is in me?*

And what do I know about living as if He does believe *in me?* Nothing can possibly separate us from the love of God that is in Christ Jesus. *And yet I doubt?* Wasn't that cross on my wrist Jesus' sign of believing in even me—because He loved me, even though all my best things are still like filthy rags (Isaiah 64:6), because He loved me enough to die on that cross even for the likes of me, because He now lives in my own broken heart me? Jesus calls us to the abundant life because He knows He can empower and fill us with His Spirit. And if He believes in us, because He Himself is actually in us, and what can be given through us—*Himself*—how can I not believe?

Jesus didn't just calm one storm—He can calm all our storms.

Jesus sings grace in the wind, He pours mercy out like rain, He grows abundance up through the broken cracks of things like wheat, and a bruised reed He will not break, and a smoldering wick He will not snuff out. And He comes as a sign to us, a sign of the cross, a sign God's reaching for us, believing in us, in love, in redemption, in making all things new, in making us enough because *He is.*

"Come, follow Me—come, I believe in you—*because I've come to live in you.*"

Real life is happening, and it's happening *right now.*

What if instead of waiting for good enough things to happen to us, we could be the good thing to happen to someone else who's waiting?

What if instead of sitting in life's waiting room, waiting for a chance for something good enough to happen to check off a bucket list—*what if abundant living isn't about what you can expect from life, but what life can expect from you?*

What if the point of everything is simply this?

Change your life expectations to focus on what life expects from you—and your life changes.

The world is brokenhearted and full of suffering, and if you listen to what life needs instead of what you need from it, you could fill the brokenness with your own brokenhearted love—and this will in turn fill you.

What if you were not afraid?

If you spend your life striving trying to get more, is that the way you actually end up with less?

Who needs more when He's already made us enough?

Why not let the heart grow big with a love large enough that it breaks your heart and gives bits of you away? And maybe this is how your soul truly gets fed anyway?

Isn't that the running dare, not to fly somewhere else to find enough, but to be like Elijah's ravens to bring people bread, to believe you could carry enough, carry Him, carry God? To be His givenness, just five minutes to Give It Forward Today, to *be the gift*—who doesn't have five minutes to become a gift? And what if doing that gave you the gift you'd been hungering for yourself?

The underbelly of the sky's scraping low and dark across the horizon, across the tops of trees, torn open. The rain's driving hard now against the window.

Exhilaration isn't in experiences themselves, but in exalting Christ Himself, in expending everything for Christ.

Before you blink and your one life's a tendril of smoke, a memory, a vapor, gone, know this: you are where you are for such a time as this—*not to make an impression, but to make a difference.* We aren't here to one-up one another, but to help one another up.

Transcend this life by giving yourself for someone else.

Maybe that's how you peel back everything that distracts and cheapens and derails a life.

Viktor Frankl, Auschwitz survivor and author of *Man's Search for Meaning*, says meaning comes when one does something that "points, and is directed, to something, or someone, other than oneself . . . by giving himself to a cause to serve or another person to love."

Experiencing the whole world will not fill your bucket like experiencing *giving yourself*, and finding the meaning that will fill your soul.

Every soul wants more than a powerful experience. It wants to experience a powerful connection.

More than being in awe, what the soul seeks is intimacy with the Other.

More than profoundly astonished, we want to be profoundly attached.

Communion, *koinonia*, is the miracle.

More than seeing and experiencing something beautiful, we want to be fully seen and experienced by Someone.

More than intimately knowing wonders, we want to know the wonder of being intimately known.

I wonder if this is the language of rain falling over broken places.

What if living the abundant life isn't about having better stories to share but about living a story that lets others live better? What if the goal isn't to experience more of the world but for more of the world to experience *more*?

EMPTY, POURED-OUT BUCKETS ARE
ACTUALLY THE FULLEST BUCKETS.

Isn't giving love sometimes infinitely easier than receiving it? Does chronic soul amnesia make me keep forgetting that if He believes in me, I am enough, because He is enough and He is within me? All I feel is I don't deserve love like this— and I don't. It's a gift, and in the pure givenness, there's pure communion. I yelled at a kid this morning. A son needed a ride into town, and I sighed too loud and said *not* today. I didn't read aloud tonight, and a little girl went to bed a bit shattered.

I know my Farmer husband can feel it, without need of words, my regrets knotted right deep into me.

Why are you afraid to be loved?

The Farmer's kneeling down in front of me with my filthy feet in his work-etched hands. There's a kind of mutual surrender necessary to communion, this decision made to receive the pouring out that I hadn't realized before. He cups my bare feet. Everywhere, there can be a willingness to be given. Everywhere, there can be the possibility of a vulnerable communion. Koinonia *is always, always the miracle.*

This could be us. The sky could widen with hope over us, the trials but stones on the way, and all the stones but steps higher up and deeper into God. We could be filled on the comfort food not of the world but the Word, enclosed in the broken-and-given of a vulnerable communion, and Love Himself would make us into love.

We could be buckets poured out and crushed into bread to feed the busted, the lonely, the least, the longing, and the lost.

That right there would be our love song.

Real love looks like a sacrificing Savior. That's the holy truth.

"This is how we know what love is: Jesus Christ laid down his life for us. And we ought to lay down our lives for our brothers and sisters" (1 John 3:16).

Love is not always agreement with someone, but it is always sacrifice for someone.

Love only has logic, only has meaning, when it takes the form of the cross.

Practice brokenness and givenness and a bit of the kingdom is here now.

You do something great with your life when you do all
the small things with His great love.

That black-inked cross, the one daily written on my
wrist, it might cut into me like a tender surgery, break me and
remake me, re-form me cruciform.

It all seemed embarrassingly small, how I ended up daily being the GIFT: complimenting an insecure kid, doing a messy chore, making a tired man's bed, taping a scrawled love note to a smudged and splattered mirror.

Why hadn't somebody showed up a long time ago in a three-piece suit to tell me those small acts of intentional love actually trigger the brain's receptor networks for oxytocin, the soothing hormone of maternal bonding? That little acts of large love actually release dopamine, that hormone associated with positive emotions and a natural high? Why hadn't anyone told me: bend low in small acts of love, and you get literally "high"?

Real love dares you to the really dangerous: *die in the diminutive*. Be broken and given in the small, the moments so small no one may applaud at all. Pour out your life in laundry rooms and over toilets and tubs, and pour out life on the back streets, in the back of the room, back behind the big lights. Pour out your life in small moments—because it's only these moments that add up to the monumental. The only way to live a truly remarkable life is not to get everyone to notice you, but to leave noticeable marks of His love everywhere you go.

Love is so large that it has to live in the holiness of very small moments of sacrifice.

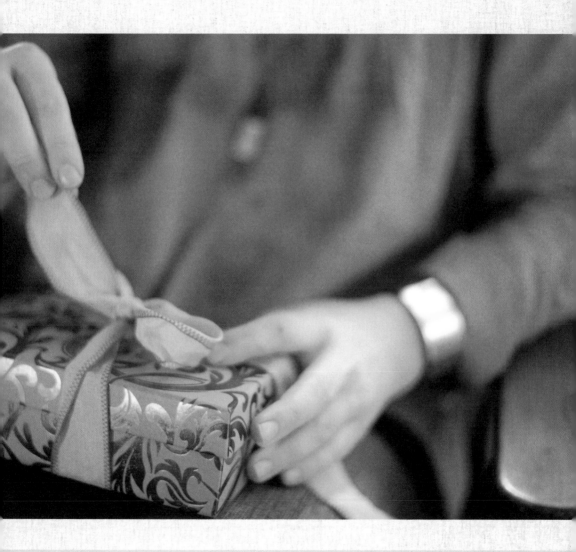

Shalom's freckles are awash in morning sun, and she's drinking down orange juice and the boys are arguing loud and heatedly over the periodic table. And Hope's looking out at morning coming across the fields, and I want to reach out and touch her—*we're all worth the risk of any brokenness.*

That canvas of the crucified Christ hangs up in the gable over the table. This vulnerable communion is a risk. Givenness is a risk. *The only way to abundant life is the broken way of risk.*

When Dad had called over this morning, he'd said his farming friend, Alan Bertrand, in his signature denim coveralls and a worn-

> To love at all is to be vulnerable. Love anything, and your
> heart will certainly be wrung and possibly be broken.
>
> —C. S. LEWIS

through cap, was "just trying to figure out whether to spend the years he's got left restoring another one of those antique tractors he has out in the shop"—he'd sighed—"or if he should spend the time he's got left, the years he still had, trying to track down his daughter he hasn't seen or heard from in ten years."

I could see Dad in my mind in his suspender overalls. "And so, Alan decided?"

"The tractor."

But—

You are whatever you love.

You are, at your very essence, not what you think, but what you love. Open up God's love letter to us—He says we're all lovers compelled by our loves. We are all compelled not by what we believe is right, *but by what we love the most.* You are not driven by duties, you are not driven by doctrines; you are driven by what you ultimately desire—*and maybe you don't actually really love whatever you think you love?*

And the saddest of all may be when we give away our lives to insignificant things, things we didn't realize we subconsciously loved. Turns out—we give our lives to things we never would if we got honest and thought about them for one single moment. It's happening every moment—our unintentional, accidental lives betray our true loves and what we subconsciously believe.

The cross on my wrist is asking me, forming me cruciform, forming me into what I say I love. This is no small thing. Because nobody's ideals form them like their loves form them.

We are made into what we make habits.

Love is a risk that's never a risk.

I didn't know how to tell Dad that, couldn't stop shaking my head. None of what he was saying made sense. *And yet it did. I knew how it did because I'd lived it.*

Dad had said it with this pain in his chest that I could feel in my own: *"There are no guarantees with people."*

And before I could think, the words had left my mouth. "Jesus said, 'Whoever loses their life for me will find it.'"

Jesus risked Himself on me. *How can I not risk my life on you?*

It's the longing for a comfortable safety that stands between you and everything you really long for.

Looking across that table at those kids scarfing down breakfast, looking into the faces of my own risk, like Alan Bertrand and Dad and the thousands who've come before, my own heart's pounding like a willing offering:

I am what I love and I will love you like Jesus, because of Jesus, through the strength of Jesus. I will love when I'm not loved back. I will love when I'm hurt and disappointed and betrayed and inconvenienced and rejected. I simply will love, no expectations, no conditions, no demands. *Love is not always agreement with someone, but it is always sacrifice for someone.*

A day is a pocket of possibility and it's always there, waiting for your willing hand.

Honestly—I don't know how to be what anyone needs me to be. I don't know how to become cruciform.

But maybe life isn't overwhelming when we simply understand how to give, just in this moment. I don't know— maybe all there is to living, to loving, is to live into the givenness of the moment.

Hope looks like she just needed arms to hold her. "Attention is the rarest and purest form of generosity," is what Simone Weil said.

"You're kind of scared about everything you've got ahead of you?" I say it into her hair quietly.

She nods, and I pull her closer, and she's so much like me and what if she ends up taking my ways of quiet desperation and I have no idea if I'm doing anything right and *what in the world am I so afraid of*? I can see the laundry on the line in the orchard, giving itself to the wind, pockets turned out and surrendered.

You are to pay special attention to those who, by accidents of time, or place, or circumstances, are brought into closer connection with you.

— AUGUSTINE

I can feel Hope breathing slow, feel my stress ebb, feel it in the warmth between us. We all long for the belonging of communion and yet there's this fear of the closeness of the fellowship. Love breaks us vulnerably open—and then can break us with rejection. There's this craving for genuine communion— and yet this fear of losing genuine independence. Need can be a terrifying thing. I know—I've built my fair share of fortress walls. You can crave communion but fear being used or manipulated or smothered or burned. I have used a thousand buckets to douse any spark of a terrifying, vulnerable communion.

How can I keep forgetting? Write it up my arms: koinonia *is always, always the miracle.*

Maybe the cross penned on my wrist is pressing the possibility of new ways of meaning and being and transforming right into the bone of things.

"There are very few men who realize what God would make of them if they abandoned themselves into His hands and let themselves be formed by His Grace," wrote Ignatius. What would happen if the abandoned abandoned themselves into His heart and let themselves be formed by His cross?

Give It Forward Today—give numerous small gifts forward today, and you get the miraculous gift of less stress. Abandon yourself to the givenness of God, and you abandon a bit of the fears and the stress.

Busy is a choice. Stress is a choice. Giving yourself to joy is a choice. Choose well.

"For in self-giving, if anywhere, we touch a rhythm not only of all creation but of all being," wrote C. S. Lewis.

Maybe it is better to give than to receive because it's only when we give that we receive what we truly need. Letting that settle into me starts to reshape the broken places.

Love will always make you suffer. Love only asks, "Who am I willing to suffer for?" This is the severe grace of love making me real. Real love is patient and it bites its tongue. It lets its heart be broken like bread.

Love isn't about feeling *good* about others; love is ultimately being willing to *suffer* for others.

LOVE IS OUR DEEPEST LONGING—AND
WHAT WE MOST DEEPLY FEAR.

PICKING UP YOUR CROSS FEELS MOST LIKE *PATIENCE*.

And if I miss that Christianity is about passionate, suffering, patient love, I've missed its essence. For the love of Christ, you can dream about starting a soup kitchen or opening an orphanage or doing some world-igniting work that will usher in utopia. But someone, somewhere, sometime, is going to let you down. Someone's not going to show up like you need them to, someone's going to complain that you're not fair, that you can't do that, and somebody's going to make it clear that you've got it really wrong. There are Job's buddies in every crowd. There's suffering around every corner, lurking in every act of love.

And if you can't bear ingratitude from the world—you can't bear love out into the world.

The moment you're most repelled by someone's heart is when you need to draw closer to that heart.

Pick up your cross. It's the only way you or anyone else can know a resurrection.

You become real when you make every situation, every suffering, every single moment, into a way to lead you into closer communion with Christ. *A broken way.*

Maybe all that matters is that we're owned by Christ and Love owns us all. That cross on my wrist, it's pointing the broken way through. It's not just telling me what to do; it's ultimately confirming Who is in me.

Trust Him in all this brokenness. *It is a gift.*

What could happen if we all weren't afraid of passion—of suffering?

MAYBE WHOLENESS IS EMBRACING
BROKENNESS AS PART OF YOUR LIFE.

More. *There is always more.* We are living in His kingdom and His endless abundance of enough, of more than enough. If we'll but surrender to givenness.

And I will fall in love and fail at love and fall in my love, but I will never stop the practicing, practicing, practicing, the givenness and the receiving. For what is faith, what is love, if it is not practiced? We in this vulnerable communion of brokenness and givenness, will simply keep surrendering again to love because God is love and this is all that wins. Maybe it's only the veneer of things that makes this look like a warring world because, at its core, this is really a world begging to be wooed. We are all lovers compelled by love. Love or war, the answer is one and the same: *I surrender.*

Given.

Impossible things are healing here, healing us all under this roof. Giving away the heart heals the heart.

I'd spent the afternoon with Mama at her place in town.

Sometimes you can hear it—the resonance between the drumming of your own pulse and the pulse of grace rising up to you from the darkest places. There is no fear in letting tears come. Rain always brings growth.

An old card lies open on the table in front of her. It's my handwriting from grade school, this blotting inky scrawl, cramped and haunting from decades ago.

"I don't want to hurt you, but I am sad and angry."

I don't remember writing the words, but I remember feeling them. Words I couldn't say about the pain that nearly claimed us both.

She bites her lip like a steadying, like a woman reaching for a hand. "You can't know how . . . how I'm far more sad for what won't ever be now."

Maybe life always tastes a bit like regret. Whatever you do or don't do, there is no way to never taste it. She's my mama, and I'm her daughter.

Make Him present—even where it feels too broken.

It hurts to swallow.

By believing against all odds and loving against all odds, that is how we are to let Jesus show in the world and to transform the world.

—FREDERICK BUECHNER

"Mama?" Her cheek feels like wrinkled silk. "Please hear me. All that was intended to harm, God intended all of it for good. All that's been, no matter what was intended to harm you, God's arms have you."

Not one of us is ever too broken. "Give our Lord the benefit of believing that His hand is leading you, and accept the anxiety of feeling yourself in suspense and incomplete," assures Pierre Teilhard de Chardin.

Without even thinking, my fingers find my wrist where I once cut, and the tips of me trace that cross, and even Joseph's suffering was the door into discovering more of God. Suffering that does not break us away from more of this world and break us into more of God is wasted suffering.

Become that cross. Cruciform.

"Mama? You and me?" And words come out from some long-ago place. "All that's been is what makes us velveteen. All that's been is what makes you beautiful, makes you love, makes you real. Remember real, Mama?"

"What is REAL?" asked the Rabbit one day . . .

"Real isn't how you are made," said the Skin Horse. "It's a thing that happens to you . . ."

"Does it hurt?" asked the Rabbit.

"Sometimes," said the Skin Horse, for he was always truthful. "When you are Real you don't mind being hurt." (Margery Williams, *The Velveeten Rabbit*)

What is real?

"My velveteen mama." I touch her cheek. "The miracle of real happens when you let all your suffering create love. When you let the pain make passion. The passion makes you real, Mama." I'm talking to her, but I'm the aching, busted one preaching gospel to myself, trying to find the way myself. I'm reading her eyes. Holding her wrinkled cheek in my hand. "I want you to be okay."

Mama nods—closing her eyes a bit like a dam to hold it all back. "Want you to be okay too, girl."

"But you know what, Mama?" I kneel down in front of her,

look up to her, her hand gently patting mine, her lips pursed trying to stop the tears. "You're teaching me how to feel safe when I'm not okay, how to feel safe when I'm un-okay . . . how to feel how I'm beloved even when I'm broken."

The penned cross on my wrist is touching Mama's wet cheek.

You are the most loved not when you're pretending to have it all together; you are actually the most loved when you feel broken and falling apart.

And maybe I'm just beginning to see?

I wipe the smudged cross off Mama's cheek.

There is a cross that makes us all safe. Jesus is drawn to the broken parts of us we would never want to draw attention to. Jesus is the most attracted to the busted and sees the broken as the most beautiful. And our God wants the most unwanted parts of us most. "Heart-shattered lives ready for love don't for a moment escape God's notice . . . The sacrifice pleasing to God is a broken spirit" (Psalm 51:17 MSG, HCSB).

Nothing pleases God more than letting Him touch the places you think don't please Him. God is drawn to broken things—so He can draw the most beautiful things.

I look up at Mama. We're doing it. We are all doing it. Picking up our crosses continuously. Making Christ present against the lies, right in the midst of brokenness . . . *Believe there is powerfulness in your brokenness.*

I stroke Mama's cheek, whisper it again like a lullaby, rocking us mother and child, rocking us two old mamas. "It's the brokenhearted passion like His that's making us real, Mama."

Sometimes it isn't your fault. Life breaks us. The fall breaks us. The brokenness inside of us breaks us. These failures and relapses and suffering and sacrifice and service, all our little-deaths, this is the painful grace that can make the willing velveteen real.

Mama and I are ringed in this fragile *koinonia*, this broken giving and receiving.

"Mama? Your heart's beautiful—especially the broken edges where you let the love get in."

She leans forward, kisses my forehead, like healing grace.

I never expected to get so much wrong. I never expected love like this. I never expected so much joy. *Be patient with God's patient work in you.*

The cross alone is what makes impossible things poss*able*.

It's not that your heart isn't going to break; it's how you let the brokenness be made into abundance afterward.

You are broken and you don't have to pretend you are not. What a relief. You begin to break your brokenness when you break down with your brokenness—when you hand it over to the One broken for you.

If repentance isn't a daily part of your life, how is grace a daily part of your life?

Repentance is what keeps turning you around, around, sanding you down, re-forming you, remaking you—making you into real.

The joy of the Lord happens inside the sorrow.

—TIMOTHY KELLER

Brokenness is always the beginning. Repentance, good brokenness, is the only way to progress in the Christian life because growth only happens through the seed broken open. You've never stood in the majesty of an oak that didn't come from a busted seed.

When you commit to loving someone, you commit to losing some of you—you commit to dying.

Is this why the vulnerable communion can feel terrifying?

In the raw experience of "I cannot do this," you experience how He remakes you into someone who can. And our broken hearts are called to that impossible, because that is who He, He who is in us, makes us: the imposs*ables.*

Love is really love—when we are loving the unlovable. Faith is really faith—when we believe God for the unbelievable.

And the cross alone is the good brokenness that can break bad brokenness and make you real.

It definitely gets harder before it gets easier. But it will definitely get better—if you don't give up when it's hardest. "So let's not allow ourselves to get fatigued doing good. At the right time we will harvest a good crop if we don't give up, or quit" (Galatians 6:9 MSG).

Grace can strike when you are in great pain and light you with the greatest hope.

> If today were your last, would you do what you're doing? Or would you love more, give more, forgive more? Then do so! Forgive and give as if it were your last opportunity. Love like there's no tomorrow, and if tomorrow comes, love again.
>
> —MAX LUCADO

She had shown me how to knit the sleeves for a sweater. Her bald head was like a pearl.

We had dinner once with her uncle Joe and her mom and dad in that Italian restaurant up in Michigan, and her dad asked the waiter to turn off the music because we were the only ones there. And those million emails, ten million messages, and a handful of girls' weekends where we made the time for each other, gave each other the gift of each other, and all laughed like hyenas over steaming Chinese takeout and cried late at night over kids and motherhood and what it means to never stop this laboring and delivering. And Elizabeth, always the GIFTer, always giving it forward today and every day, finished knitting those matching socks for all four of us. We didn't know how we'd ever walk away from each other.

She died on Maundy Thursday, the Thursday He mandated for us to love one another, the Thursday of communion. Koinonia *is always, always the miracle.* I

can hear her voice on the other end of the line and how she would say it always unashamed: *"I love you."*

Why do we not say what we mean until it's too late for it to mean anything? I can close my eyes and hear her laugh. Quick— open your eyes and see everything you can, memorize everything you can, before you can never open your eyes again.

This is all I can do now to try to keep loving her: I can show up. Show up for her family. Show up for her funeral. Elizabeth would have loved that. Would she have loved it if I had showed up more? Showed up with the gift of an old frayed blanket and told her—not asked her, but told her—that we were going to the park with a stack of old books to watch the clouds? If I had called her back that time I thought it was too late? If I hadn't walked by that scarf that was screaming her name and surprised her with it as a just-because gift?

If I'd stolen five minutes, grabbed a postcard, and scrawled out three lines—"There isn't a laugh in the world like yours. You handed me a life supply of courage because you loved me like this. And yeah, you pretty much beat me at everything, but I win at this: I love you more." Why hadn't I been that gift more often? The ministry of presence is a gift with an expiry date. Everything proves it now: this is unexpected happiness, to be broken and given to bless.

The priest steps into the carved pulpit, his robes whispering. His voice is unhurried, like old wine, full-bodied and settled. He says last he sat with Elizabeth, she'd murmured, "I give this all up

to You." The words echo through the vaulting space. How does it change everything to read suffering as Christ's invitation to follow Him to the cross and share His cross? "Christ goes to the cross, and we are invited to follow to the same cross. Not because it is the cross, but because it is His," writes Peter Kreeft.

Be brave and do not pray for the hard thing to go away, but pray for a bravery that's bigger than the hard thing.

Elizabeth tells me once, tells me a dozen times, especially in the middle of her cancer-wracking nights: the longer she suffers, the longer she gets to love. This is always true, everywhere. Elizabeth didn't avoid suffering, because she didn't want to avoid loving.

Because Elizabeth knew "love is the most characteristic and comprehensive act of the human being." As Eugene Peterson continued, "We are most ourselves when we love; we are most the People of God when we love," and loving like Jesus loves, embodying our union with Christ and our *koinonia* with the body of Christ—*this* is the singular life work of the Jesus follower.

This is always worth the suffering.

I stand by her casket, feeling what she knew: grief is the guaranteed price we always pay for love.

THIS IS HOW YOU LIVE WITH YOUR ONE
BROKEN HEART: YOU GIVE IT AWAY.

The way through brokenness is, and always has been, to break the sufferer free from the aloneness of the suffering by choosing to participate in the suffering with them—*koinonia*—choosing to stand with the suffering, stay with the suffering, and let it all be shaped into meaning that *transcends* the suffering. He is Immanuel—our God who is with us.

Elizabeth had asked me to sit with her through the cold of the chemo. She had tried to knit socks through the drip—more prayer socks, praying through every loop. She had chosen it: Be a prayer warrior. Not a panicked worrier.

I look up and down the pews. Rainbows of socks. People have worn the socks that Elizabeth knitted for them—Elizabeth's prayer socks, her prayers knit into every single one of the 19,800 stitches in a pair of socks. The pews are filled with them, a kaleidoscope of teals and purples, misty blues and greys and a riot of cerulean—shod in scuffed-up Mary Janes and patented ballet flats, sneakers, and polished black loafers. We are all shod in the gospel, in bits of Elizabeth, broken and given and knit together, and I could break down right here.

A violin plays. A cello. Wine, the cup of His suffering, it stings hot and dangerous down my willing throat. That's what Elizabeth did. She became wine, dangerous to my protective, barrier walls. You can't know the wine you will be during the days you are breaking and being crushed like grapes.

Are the most painful chapters of our lives always the most meaningful?

We can receive it if we want—*there is always more God.* In tears is intimacy. God understands because He stands with us. Hundreds of us stand shoulder to shoulder in our holy socks in the church sanctuary, giving everything in our lungs. *Thou in me dwelling, and I with Thee one.* There is always union with Christ that we only need wake to and *koinonia* always is the miracle. I try to memorize everything—the colors, the faces, all the eyes. *Heart of my own heart, whatever befall . . .*

I had read it and never forgotten: the word *suffer* comes from the Latin "to bear under." Suffering is an act of surrender, to bear under that which is not under our control. I want to ask Elizabeth: *Is this why we avoid suffering at all costs? Is this why we desperately try to avoid pain, because suffering is a surrender to the uncontrollable?*

Suffering asks us to bear under that which is ultimately not under our control, which proves to us we have no control. And maybe that's too much for us in our autonomous, do-it-yourself culture to bear. Maybe more than we can't stand physical suffering, we can't stand not feeling in control.

TO BE THE RE-MEMBERING PEOPLE—
THIS IS THE WORK OF LIFE IN A
BROKENHEARTED WORLD.

We are all a body, we belong to one another, we are one. This is the practical reality. Relationship is the only real reality. Unless our everyday reality reflects the practical reality of our oneness, we live a horror story of distortion and dis-memberment. To be the re-membering people—this is the work of life in a brokenhearted world.

I look up and the moment is weightless, lifted in a spiral of candle flame underneath the big cross on the wall. *Do this in re-membrance of Me.* Anything less than living out the reality of the oneness of the body is illusion and ends in insanity.

How do you know how to hold space for all this brokenness and not be afraid? This cross on my wrist—it's been showing me how to hold pain, to hold the pain of little deaths. To not be afraid of it, to not fight it. The cross allows you to hold pain—because that cross is absorbing all your pain.

On the way home, a man named Lorne looks like he needs help finding his way. I stop, ask how I can help. He shows me the name of what he's looking for, asks me the time. His face is a dawning light of realization in me when he nods good-bye.

I take an extra minute later to tell a cashier how she's gold medaling in service with a smile. Her eyes shimmer, instantly familiar. I stop and whisper to a kid reading a book on a street bench—readers like her are the next world changers—and I wait for the light. I get to be the gift still, to give it forward, to break and give away all the love Elizabeth gave to me. I look into the eyes of people all the way home.

And for a string of moments, I remember that I get to live into the dare that though there is suffering in this world, though there is dying of the loveliest and most loved, though shards of our broken hearts pierce our lungs' every breath, there's the grace of a miraculous communion of all the broken. There's the dare to come to the feast to be shared.

Teach us to number our days, that we may gain a heart of wisdom.

—PSALM 90:12

> Faith is a
> living, daring
> confidence in
> God's grace,
> so sure and
> certain that a
> man could stake
> his life on it a
> thousand times.
>
> —MARTIN
> LUTHER

Elizabeth is gone. And I've failed to love like I've wanted to. Always, I'd about give my eye teeth and left arm for more time to get it more deeply right and less painfully wrong. I wanted to be more—more patient, to never lose it, to always have it together, to keep calm and sane. I've wanted more flashes of wisdom in the heat of the moment when I had no bloody idea what was the best thing to do. I've wanted fewer nights crawling into bed feeling like a failure who always gets it wrong when everyone else seems to get it right. I've wanted to take the gold medal in living well and loving large and being enough to be wanted. Instead, I've been the person who escapes behind bathroom doors, the person who turns on the water so no one can hear the howl, the person who fights what is and struggles to surrender, who completely ups and forgets how to break into givenness.

Maybe the only way to begin breaking free is to lay open your willing hands and bear witness to the ugly mess of your scars. To trace them slowly and re-member what He says about you, even if you forget. This is about bravely letting our darkness be a canvas for God's light. *This happened that the glory of God might be shown through even you.*

What if the re-membering of your brokenness comes in remembering that your trying isn't what matters the most, because His scars have written your name and your worth over all of yours?

He went without comfort so that you might have it. He postponed joy so that you might share in it. He willingly chose isolation so that you might never be alone in your hurt and sorrow.

—JONI EARECKSON TADA

What if I fully surrendered to becoming cruciform so I could feel along my scars, along my own scarred face, and know my own name is Beloved? I don't know if there's any other way to break into abundant living unless I come to *know* this.

> Christians who understand biblical truth and have the courage to live it out can indeed redeem a culture, or even create one.
>
> —CHUCK COLSON

This man is standing penniless and parched in my kitchen. My brother has brought him. His name is Gordon, and he's asked for a glass of water. And I've stood in a kitchen of sorts in a dump in Guatemala City and looked into the whites of kids' eyes eating whatever they could find in piles of rotting refuse, the vultures circling overhead. And I've stood at a chain-link fence in Haiti when a small boy appeared out of nowhere, the barren foothills bloating malnourished up behind him as he rattled the fence with one dirty hand and pointed to his cracked lips, begging for food—even a sip of water.

You can look into eyes and hear the whisper from those outside your door, outside the gate: You've got to risk your position inside for those on the outside or you risk losing everything, even your own soul. You've got to give your gifts or they may become your idols, your identity, and you become the walking dead.

If your living isn't about giving, then you're already dying.

There are so many of us sucking down lattes and dying of thirst, dying for something more, for something abundant. There are so many in need, and so many Esthers who thirst for more than vanilla services, sweetened programs, and watered-down lives, hungry for some real meat for their starved souls, some dirt under the fingernails, some real sacrifice in the veins. I know why I keep writing a cross on my wrist.

There's a whole generation of Esthers who want to be the gift, want to give it forward, whatever's in our hands, who want holy more than hollow. There's a whole Esther Generation, and it is we who want the abundant life of going lower to love the least, the lonely, and the lost. The world needs people who will defy cynical indifference by making a critical difference.

Every one of us can start changing headlines when we start reaching out our hands.

We can be concerned for the poor—but be no less concerned for us rich who claim not to be rich so we can excuse ourselves from giving. Go ahead and show concern for the poor—but be no less concerned if we've merely done enough to assuage our consciences, just enough to pat ourselves on the back, but not enough that we've ever felt true sacrifice, that we've ever actually *broken* and given. Go ahead and live concerned for the poor—but be no less concerned for avoiding suffering because someday we will face Christ. What if caring for the poor was more than just caring about easing our consciences? What if caring for the poor may mean sacrifice, and what if this is the way to be *satisfied* and know abundant living?

"*To do justice,*" writes Tim Keller, "means to go to places where the fabric of shalom has broken down, where the weaker members of societies are falling through the fabric, and to repair it."

We are each singular threads in the world. We all get to decide what we will tie our lives to. If I tie my resources, my time, my Esther-power, only to the thin thread of my own life—my life's a hopelessly knotted mess.

The thread of your life becomes a tapestry of abundant colors only if it ties itself to other lives. The only way to strengthen the fabric of society is to let threads of your life break away to let Christ, who is in us, weave around other threads. "Reweaving shalom means to sacrificially thread, lace, and press your time, goods, power, and resources into the lives and needs of others . . . The strong must disadvantage themselves for the weak, the majority for the minority, or the community frays and the fabric breaks."

The only way to care for the disadvantaged is to disadvantage yourself, *which is guaranteed to turn out to your advantage.*

We're all been the ones outside the gate pleading for Someone to risk everything to rescue us. This could break a million little self-righteous pulpits: *the brokenness in the world is but the brokenness in our own busted hearts.*

My own busted heart's got nothing to give. But I don't need to have things together before I can offer a cup of water, open the door, my hand, or reach out to help those outside. I don't need to not be thirsty myself; I only need to know I thirst too.

Because grace is a beam that begs us to let it run on and support everything.

And it isn't *having* that makes us rich; it's *giving*. Give sacrificially, live richly. Maybe all we really want is more of God. Abundance of Him.

How many times have I missed Him? You miss Him when you question who's needy enough to give to, who warrants the risk. He comes as the homeless guy, the refugee, the child drinking filthy water—and you get to decide. Are you going to fill your life with more stuff, more safety, or more God? What the world says is weak and small may be where Christ is offering Himself to you most of all—and why do we want to be big people when God shows up as the little people nobody's got time for? You miss Jesus when you aren't looking for His two disguises: the smallest and the servant.

"The mystery of ministry is that the Lord is to be found where we minister," writes Henri Nouwen. "That is what Jesus tells us when He says: 'Insofar as you did this to one of the least of these brothers of mine, you did it to me' (Matthew 25:40). Our care for people thus becomes the way to meet the Lord. The more we give, help, support, guide, counsel, and visit, the more we receive, not just similar gifts, but the Lord himself. To go to the poor is to go to the Lord."

I get back from Iraq, where I sat with women who witnessed genocide, and at church somebody tells me, "It's nice that you care about those people over there." And I stop. Turn. How do I translate it? We aren't where we are to care about those on the margins—some nice gesture or token concern. I look across the kitchen at Gordon. The reason we are here is to risk everything for those oppressed people *over there* outside the gate. You are where you are to help others where they are. This isn't a Christian's sideline hobby; compassion is our complete vocation. We do not just care about people; caring is our calling. That's it.

God forbid, you don't get a roof over your head and food on your table because you deserve more, but so you can serve more. God forbid, you believe you're a little better than others instead of making another's life a little better.

NEVER BE AFRAID OF
BROKEN THINGS—BECAUSE CHRIST IS
REDEEMING EVERYTHING.

I could hear the cautions in my head: Is this safe? *But what is love if not this? Real love is never safe.* When it comes to real love, there is safety in living Christ's dangerous call. How many times have I thought it was safety that mattered, when Jesus already died to save us? No one ever got saved unless someone else was willing to be unsafe. Some notion of safety isn't what ultimately matters; what matters is: *If we see someone in need and don't help in some way, isn't that in some way sin?* Love of strangers— wasn't that the direct, exact translation of the word for hospitality in Scripture, *philoxenia*? *Philos*—brotherly love; *xenia*—the stranger. Love the stranger like a brother. Biblical hospitality is about inviting strangers in, not just the neighbors.

"When you give a lunch or a dinner, don't invite your friends, your brothers, your relatives, or your rich neighbors, because they might invite you back, and you would be repaid. On the contrary, when you host a banquet, invite those who are poor, maimed, lame, or blind. And you will be blessed, because they cannot repay you." (Luke 14:12–14 HCSB)

Give the gift forward to the stranger who cannot repay you, to those outside the gate, so the only repayment is the abundance of God. The sun's spilling down the old wooden barn ladder I'd placed by the kitchen table. Grace is always a movement of downward mobility.

The world changes when we don't categorize, polarize, and demonize people with broad brushstrokes—but when we apologize, empathize, evangelize, and prioritize people with these quiet brushes of grace.

Maybe we don't live abundantly until we let others break into us—the foster child who needs a break, the angry teenager, the guy we can't stand, the neighbor who is always complaining, the people on the other side of the gate, till everyone who crosses your path breaks a bit into your heart. Their vulnerabilities become ours, their prayers become ours, their hopes become ours. Love bears all things and we are the Esthers who bear *whatever it takes* for those outside the gate.

We belong to each other because we all mutually indwell each other, and there is nothing worth having inside the gate when we've got pieces of ourselves outside the gate. When we leave people on the other side of the gate—*we lose parts of ourselves.*

WE WILL BE KNOWN FOR OUR ACTUAL FRUITS,
NOT THE INTENTIONS OF OUR IMAGINATIONS.

The way to slowly die is to believe you live in a space of scarcity and not abundance of generosity. The abundant way to life is the paradox of the broken way, to believe we live with enough time, enough resources, enough God. Any fear of giving to God's kingdom is flawed. It would be like a farmer who feared losing his bucket of seeds so he failed to plant his own field—and thus forfeited the joy of overflowing his barns with the harvest.

From the table, you can see the Mason jar of wheat seeds in the windowsill. There's always enough abundance and grace to risk everything for those in need, because you have the favor of the King and it's only by abundant grace that any of us are here—and if there's abundant grace for us, by God, there's abundant grace for all of us.

There isn't a barrier in the world that can block out pain. There isn't a wall you can build that protects you from pain. Addiction, escapism, materialism, anger, indifference—none of these can stop pain—and each one creates a pain all its own. *There is no way to avoid pain. There is no way to avoid brokenness. There is absolutely no way but a broken way.*

Barriers that falsely advertise self-protection are guaranteed ways of self-imprisonment. Barriers that supposedly will protect your heart so it won't break are guaranteed to break your heart anyway.

Yet being brave enough to lay your heart out there to be broken, to be rejected in a thousand little ways, this may hurt like a kind of hell—but it will be holy. The only way in the whole universe to find connection . . . is to let your heart be broken. Love only comes to those brave enough to risk being brokenhearted.

It's when we defend our hearts and are deaf to the cries of other hearts that the world becomes absurd—*surdus* in Latin, which means "deaf." The absurdity of hurt only changes when we stop being deaf and begin to *listen* to each other's hearts. *Audire* in Latin: "obedient." The way to a God-obedient life is to sincerely listen.

If we want to genuinely practice our faith, don't we need to genuinely listen? How would the world change if we all became masters in the art of hearing heartbeats? God's and His people's.

Had I known: God takes us into wildernesses not to abandon us but to be alone with us. Wildernesses are not where God takes us to hurt us—but where He speaks to our hearts. Wildernesses can be safe because we are always safe when we are always with Him. Wildernesses can be where God woos. God had wooed me—a wife of harlotry. I have cried in deserts, been revived by the caress of His grace.

And His Word can come through the trees like wind. "I was hungry and you fed me, I was thirsty and you gave me a drink, I was homeless and you gave me a room, I was shivering and you gave me clothes, I was sick and you stopped to visit, I was

HUMANITY'S PARTICULAR BEAUTY IS ONLY *POSSIBLE* BECAUSE OF ITS BRAVE FRAGILITY. LOOK TO YOUR VULNERABLE GOD.

in prison and you came to me . . . I'm telling the solemn truth: Whenever you did one of these things to someone overlooked or ignored, that was me—you did it to me" (Matthew 25:35–36, 40 MSG).

The only way to love God . . . is to give to people. Love for Him has to turn into giving, or it was never love.

The only way to love God . . . is to give to people.

The only way to serve God . . . is to serve people.

The only way to woo God . . . is to care for the wounds of people.

The only way to woo God . . . is to let Him care for your wounds and give Him your brokenhearted need.

Never be afraid of being a broken thing.

There's a chip in the handle of this teacup. I feel like I'm seeing everything for the first time.

He's inviting me to heal, but also to see my most meaningful calling: to be His healing to the hurting. My own brokenness, driving me into Christ's, is exactly where I can touch the brokenhearted. Our most meaningful purpose can be found exactly in our most painful brokenness. I'm not sure I'd known: *we can be brokers of healing exactly where we have known the most brokenness.*

Why have we swallowed the lie that we can only help if we're perfect? The cosmic truth sealed in the wounds of the broken God is that the greatest brokers of abundance know an unspoken broken. Wrapping my hands around the empty, cracked mug feels like this strange comfort. *It's all going to be okay.* What makes us feel the most disqualified for the abundant life is actually what makes us the most qualified. It's the broken and the limping, the wounded and the scarred, the stragglers and the strugglers, who may know best where to run with wounds. It's only the broken who know where the cracks are and how our broken wounds can be the very thin places that reveal God . . . and allow us to feel His safe holding hand.

Those who've known an unspoken broken can speak the most real healing.

The wounds that never heal are always the ones mourned alone. And you can tell yourself you're ready for God to heal it or use it however He wills, but that doesn't stop this quiet questioning of what it could mean or how it may feel. But you can go ahead and strap into a plane heading east, leaving the safety and comfort of home, because you're doing whatever it takes to move higher up and deeper into trusting God, what it takes to be in a different place by your next birthday, and one ten years from now.

Sometimes you don't know how wounded you are until you step out of your familiar ruts. Until you've slowed down, until you press your back up against the steadying strength of an oak tree on a humid Thursday out in some far-flung place and you look up into those tree limbs and realize half that tree is underground, and you can only see the half rooted in the light. That's when you can feel the wounded parts of you, the underground parts of you, how they'll do whatever it takes to keep reaching for the light.

I'm standing under the shade in a field in Israel, listening to a weathered man talk about sheep and the compassion of a shepherd, and the air isn't merely hot out here; it's suffocating. In the heat, that cross inked on my wrist has left a mirror image on my leg. My body being shaped cruciform. All these things inside of me taking shape: the only way to break the idols in your life is to accept what Jesus gives you freely that every other god demands but that you can never achieve. Jesus comes to *give* you freely through His passion what every other god forces you to try to *get* through performance.

I trace the little blurred cross on my leg. How can I not ache with a grateful love for a compassion like this? And how could His compassion for me not compel me to give His compassion to the aching?

Compassion isn't saccharine sentimentality; it's key to humanity's survival. Compassion heals what condemnation never could. I lap it up—what I'm parched for, what the world's parched for: Jesus is drawn to the broken with a deep compassion. Jesus is drawn to *my* deep broken with a deep compassion.

Safety is found where the brokenness of two hearts meet. The relief of it runs down into the wounds of me.

The word means "together," *com*, and "to suffer," *pati*. Compassion is about co-passion, about co-suffering. You only have compassion where you are willing to co-suffer.

How else can you make Christ's presence known apart from cruciform compassion? What if the only way to move forward in any situation is to always be moved with compassion?

It's relatively easy to pontificate on how to live the gospel; it's infinitely harder to incarnate the gospel in your life. I want to shake my own hard heart awake.

If Jesus felt compassion more than any other feeling, can we learn?

There's more abundance in daily giving your presence to one than daily diligence for the furtherance of hundreds.

Anyone can have enough compassion to write a check for the needy, but who has compassion for the kid who makes life hard?

Compassion can feel like the right thing when it involves a donation. But when there's been a violation of your rights? Compassion can feel like degradation.

No one has to holler it too loud to me—sometimes the Spirit speaks the clearest in the quiet. He's a wind and I'm a bell, rung with conviction. Everyone wants to change the world, but who wants to change the laundry over? Everyone's passionate about changing the world, but who's changing themselves to find compassion in their own world?

God help me. Literally. *God. Help. Me.*

When all else fails, those three words never fail.

Compassion is a crawling in under the skin of someone else and connecting to their heart like it's yours. Your heart breaks into theirs and your way is bound to theirs and don't tell me that's not profoundly terrifying. But it's profoundly purifying and sanctifying and God-glorifying and soul-unifying—and ultimately, life-satisfying. It's precisely through this communion of compassion that a soul finds the connectedness it seeks. Yes, it will hurt, but it will heal. Yes, you must grow weak enough to love the world, and yet strong enough to let Christ carry your cross and all the willing world's or you will be crushed by all of it. And yes, compassion says there will only be abundance for me when there is abundance for you, so I will be bread broken and given to you so we both can taste the communion of abundance.

My name on His hand. His name on mine. *I am His and He is mine.*

Is that what I'm doing with this ridiculous experiment of penning a cross on my wrist? With just those two cross strokes, it's like I am writing my way and my name and my identity: Enough. There is enough. Abundantly enough.

I am enough, because I have enough of Him and He is always enough, and that is enough for anything. I am signing my name and my identity and being signed by the Cross One, the Risen One. I am shaping my life and letting my life be shaped, writing it down into me so it literally forms me: a passionate life is a sacrificial life. A life that wants to embrace Christ is a life that must embrace suffering. A life of giving is ultimately the most life-giving. And every single time I sign that cross on my wrist, I'm guaranteeing I can always find my sign from God, pointing the way forward—*given.*

Maybe—*communion can* only happen when not only our strong parts are broken and given, but when our broken parts are also given. Maybe communion happens not only when we're broken and given—but *when we give each other our brokenness.*

My heart's beating louder than anything else I can hear. I'm feeling along the edge of something I've never fully felt: Maybe what's given out of strength can show care through our willingness to give. But everything given out of our brokenness can show greater love through our willingness to *suffer.* Any healing communion that we can give will come not through our strength, but *through our brokenness.*

THE MIRACLE HAPPENS IN THE BREAKING.

Generosity does give birth to intimacy—but there's a far deeper intimacy when we're generous in sharing our brokenness. If you can be brave enough, vulnerable enough, humble enough, trust enough, and give the most broken shards of your heart to another believing broken heart . . . then is it your own broken shards that can best open up another heart?

I wonder if that isn't what I've been waiting so long to do, to . . . break open my own heart?

While there is deep wisdom in reserving our hearts with those who don't love through Christ's broken heart, there's even deeper wisdom in trusting enough to share our broken hearts with those who do. The more we seek Christ's broken heart in others, maybe the more we will find it, and the safer we'll find we are to share our own broken hearts with them.

There is no fellowship for brokenhearted believers while protecting others from our own brokenness—because we are the fellowship of the broken . . . and fellowship happens in the brokenness. *The miracle happens in the breaking.*

I trace that cross on my wrist slowly, outline the beams. It's exactly the places of brokenness that let the need and power of the cross bleed through.

How had I tried to avoid suffering, mask my suffering, terminate all suffering instead of sharing it, letting others participate in my own, choosing to stand with others in theirs, stay with their suffering and break the heart open and let people into all of my own—so the suffering might be shaped into an intimacy that *transcends* and *transforms* the suffering? The heart has a far greater capacity for pain than can even be imagined—because it can love far greater than ever imagined.

Someone just choosing to be with you in your fire with a bit of theirs—can turn out to be better than anyone trying to extinguish your fire. Shared flames and shared burn scars can ignite hearts into a great fire that fights fire.

If you can sit in your burn and brokenness and let it break down all your walls—so you can live into the givenness of even your brokenness—the crisis can bond you to Christ and other broken hearts.

The hospital room feels like a holy kind of beauty. Like a visitation.

With-ness breaks brokenness.

God with us. He names Himself that: *Immanuel.* God with us—because with-ness breaks brokenness. God's with us in the fire. Maybe suffering doesn't have to torch life purpose but can ultimately achieve the true purpose of life—intimacy. Where suffering is shared, communion is tasted. And maybe the fellowship of the broken—*koinonia* in the brokenness—begins to mitigate that suffering. Isn't that what I could now feel— with-ness breaking brokenness?

There's a cross bleeding into my thin skin, that's with me in my veins, in my cracked heart.

You may be called by Christ to be broken and given to the world, but you only become like Christ when you give your brokenness to the world. Everyone needs communion in their brokenness and Christ always comes to us showing His scars.

I hadn't known that full cruciformity looked fully like this. To give someone your broken heart means breaking pride, breaking lies, breaking fear. There's no communion unless someone breaks their ego. All along, had I only been scratching the surface of what it meant to be broken and given? How had I not lived like the brokenness itself is a gift?

EVERYONE NEEDS SOMEONE TO BE WITH
THEM IN THE BURN. THIS CAN TURN
THE FLAMES INTO A HOLY BLAZE.

Why not embrace the life work of embracing suffering, embracing brokenness? Why avoid the gift of more God, more vulnerability, more intimacy, more communion—the gifts that brokenheartedness offers? Why had I found that terrifying to incarnate? Suffering is a call for presence; it's a call for us to be present—not only to the brokenness in the world, but to the brokenness in our own soul, and to risk trusting others with our wounds. I think that is what's terrified me—trusting others with my wounds.

If I have loved others breathing in grace, why would I deny myself the same oxygen? And if I have needed to breathe in grace for me, how can I deny anyone needing the same oxygen? Let all our brokenness be met by grace for all of us. We might breathe it in—and the pain might wane.

I reach out and barely touch my reflection in the windowpane. Judging is a blindfold. Judging others blinds us to our own grime— and to the grace that others are as needy of as we are.

Grace makes you safe.

THE WAY TO LIVE WITH YOUR ONE BROKEN HEART—IS TO GIVE IT AWAY. *WHAT YOU NEED TO GIVE IS YOUR OWN BROKENNESS.*

It's like the cross on my wrist pulses through my skin with that one word, like everything moves and falls down around and breathes and orbits and spins and unfurls and breaks free with that one word beating like a cry at the brave center of everything: *Given. Given.* Here is my brokenness. Given. Here is my battered life, here is my bruised control, here are my fractured dreams, here is my open hand, here is all that I have, here is my fragile, surrendered heart, here I am, a living sacrifice. Broken. Given.

Living given is more than giving your skills and your resources and your time and your hands and feet. Living given means breaking down all the thickened walls and barriers around your heart with this hammer of humility and trusting the expansiveness of the broken-wide-open spaces of grace and communion. *Can I do this?*

Unguarded, arms stretched out in widest surrender. Cruciform. Given. This is freedom.

I think maybe at the root of all control-wrestling and stress lies a fear of brokenness. Everything never made, never dreamed, never risked, never tried was because of a fear of brokenness. If there was too high a chance that the dream, the hope, the plan, might break, maybe it was just a failure I couldn't risk. And what made my life tight, what made my life anxious, what had made my life closed off and broken in a thousand ways, was merely that: fear of brokenness.

Everything in life that has ever been broken . . . has been because of fear of brokenness.

I want to lay my head down on something, let the emotion come.

Fear of brokenness has pushed away everything I have ever wanted, everything I have loved. It's been my very fear of brokenness that has caused unspoken brokenness. It was that: fear of brokenness has kept me from so much living; it has kept me from so much loving.

What is fear of brokenness but fear of suffering?

If I have feared brokenness, suffering, all my life . . . does that mean I have sought my own comfort more than I have sought Christ? To fear suffering can be a fear of communion. A fear of Jesus and His ways of love. Whatever's breaking up across the breadth of me hurts like relief. I could heal. Kai rolls over in the heaviness of dreams, drapes his hand from the side of the bed. I reach over, take his hand, trace the lines in his palm. Wasn't it like an offering everywhere: brokenness offers closeness.

> For as we share abundantly in Christ's sufferings, so through Christ we share abundantly in comfort too. (2 Corinthians 1:5 ESV)

> We are . . . fellow heirs with Christ, provided we suffer with him in order that we may also be glorified with him. (Romans 8:16–17 ESV)

> My goal is to know Him and the power of His resurrection and the fellowship of His sufferings, being conformed to His death. (Philippians 3:10 HCSB)

Be very glad—for these trials make you partners with Christ in his suffering, so that you will have the wonderful joy of seeing his glory when it is revealed to all the world. (1 Peter 4:13 NLT)

Without an intimate fellowship with Christ's sufferings—how can there be intimate love with Christ? Refusing to be identified with the sufferings of Christ refuses any identity in Christ. I can feel my pulse there under his. No fear of the brokenness. No fear of the brokenness. It's beating right there under that cross that's brand-marked into me, and I'm learning to listen to it more than anything else. *Given. Given. Union with Christ in sufferings, communion with Christ in all things.*

Never be afraid of broken things—because Christ is redeeming everything.

Snowflakes melt down the window in this steady cadence.

NO FEAR OF THE BROKENNESS.
THIS FEELS LIKE FREEDOM.

Oswald Chambers wrote, "God's way is always the way of suffering—the way of the 'long long trail.'" God's way is always the broken way. For all my prayers and efforts to be broken and given for the suffering of the world, there'd been parts of me still terrified of suffering, avoiding it, still resisting being surrendered and broken and given. But now that is all I want. I want to be part of this fellowship. The fellowship of the broken believe that suffering is a gift He entrusts to us and He can be trusted to make this suffering into a gift. The fellowship of the broken take up the fearless broken way, are not afraid of brokenness, and don't need to try to fix anyone's brokenness, or try to hide it or judge it or mask it or exile it. It's like my ceiling has become an open sky: I can break open my hand and my need to control because I'm no longer afraid of broken things. *Never be afraid of broken things—because Christ can redeem anything.*

I want to be part of the fellowship of the broken.

When I'm no longer afraid of brokenness, I don't have to control or possess anything—dreams or plans or people or their perceptions. I can live surrendered. Cruciform. Given. This feels like freedom.

Not being afraid of the brokenness—*this sets you free in a thousand ways.*

Free! FREE! Free to simply sit with brokenness and feel a brokenhearted Healer come closer even now, especially now, to cup the broken hearts laid out on the table.

I'd sat today in the waiting room beside a woman who told me she had just buried her husband. Lou Gehrig's disease and a protracted death wrestle. I watched her grip the armrests until her knuckles turned white and I tried to hear all the things she didn't find words for. Her open face turned to me. "I cared for him right till the end . . ." Her eyes drifted off like she'd seen behind the veil.

"This is all I know now about living: Every moment is a gift with each other—and every moment we get to be a gift to each other. *This is all there is.*"

I nodded, holding her gaze, gave forward the gift of presence—because I knew a broken story kind of like that, of one broken woman reaching out to touch the intimate communion of the cross, and finding in it the form of a life—cruciform.

Love comes down, a gift, and grateful *eucharisteo* rises back to Him. And then *koinonia* love, broken and given as the gift, reaches out to an aching world—even, especially, with bits of our broken self. *Cruciform.*

Eucharisteo had led me to *koinonia*—was it so surprising? When you feel a radical gratitude for what you have, you end up wanting to go to radical lengths to share it. When you are radically grateful for being blessed, you want to be radically generous to the oppressed. Because you know that is the way to radical abundance—there's always room for more to share the grace.

We are where we are to risk everything for those outside the gate, because we are *one* with the broken—all gates that divide us are mirage. Comfort and affluence can make you blind. Blind to the hungry Christ, the thirsty, suffering, broken Christ. Isn't this why it's hard for the comfortable to experience authentic abundance—because they're blinded to Christ?

I'd reached out my hand to hold the grieving widow's. *Willing to be broken into. Broken and given. This is all there is.* Those who claim Christ aren't only saved by a crucified Savior; their lives are *shaped* by Him.

The cross isn't some cheap symbol of faith; it's the exact shape we embody as the life of Christ. When we won't see the suffering—who are *all* of us—we never form our lives like our Savior's.

A Christ-shaped life is not a comfortably shaped life, but a cross-shaped life.

Had my own hands had to be broken free of performance, of idols, of convenience, of perfectionism, to stop being afraid to be cut or wounded, to stop fearing the suffering of broken things? Had I had to feel the depths of my own insufficiency and brokenness to allow a deeper abundance to come?

The sun dips toward the golden hour and I wander out toward the wheat because I need . . . I need to stretch out my arms and feel the whole expanse of the flung sky, the ocean of rolling wheat breaking free, feel how fear is executed with one line: *there is enough*. Run through the gilded stalks and feel how all fear shrivels when you serenade your heart with one refrain: *there is abundance*. There is always more because God is always enough, and He makes all brokenness into abundance. Never be afraid of broken things because Christ is redeeming everything. Run and feel the bowed heads open the way: "The Lord is indeed going before you—he will be with you; he will not fail you or abandon you. Do not be afraid" (Deuteronomy 31:8 NET).

The sky and a thousand cups of light break overhead:
You can abandon all your cares because Christ will never, ever
abandon you. You can abandon your fears and abide in the safe
expanse of Your Father.

The fading dome of blue sky over the gold stretches over
me, over everything, and the evening breeze exhales the secret
to relief: the soul is broken free when we're freed of self and
abandoned to the will of God.

Hope's coming across the fields to me, her hair falling long
across her shoulders, the color of wheat. The woods fall away
behind us. When she reaches me, she reaches for my hand, smiles,
and we hold on to each other and run, laughing, lifted into the
rustle of all this willing surrender making abundance.

Can I memorize her here with me, our with-ness breaking
brokenness?

Oh, this long way we'd come through brokenness is the essence of humanness, and fragility is the beating heart of humanity, and accepting that without shame is the beginning of freedom. Brokenness doesn't need shame or guilt—brokenness needs to be shared and given. Broken and given and shared with Jesus, and with a world that needs to embrace weakness to embrace abundance. She doesn't let go of my hand.

This deeper communion with God I'd been after, the question of how to live with brokenness, it's remade me, re-formed me, reshaped me—again. I am found to the extent I keep *koinonia* with the broken because He loves best those who need Him most. It's whispering through wheat and ringing loud in my soul.

What do you do with your brokenness? Give your one broken heart away. *What's the answer to suffering in this world?* Destroy it with co-suffering, with compassion, with givenness. Bad brokenness is always broken by good brokenness. Your life turns around when you refuse to turn away from brokenness.

Once you dare to take the broken way, stay with the broken, daily give forward even your brokenness, your broken heart is enlightened, it becomes light.

Hope keeps Turning, finding my eyes, smiling, and I hold her hand tighter, her a blazing Esther, giving herself and risking loving me, even me. Sun's broken into the wheat, indwells all the wheat, and we're running straight into all the light, the heads of wheat brushing the scars on my wrist, the cross on my wrist, her hand in mine, a blur of scars, thousands upon thousands of bowed heads ready to yield breathing it: *Givenness. Givenness.*

This is communion. This is freedom. Union with Him, with His Beloved. And there is no stopping the breaking free. I could trust enough to give, give Him forward, give even my own brokenness, and not be afraid it would break anyone—because brokenness makes communion. Brokenness makes abundance. The aloneness and disconnect and abandonment felt from the beginning, it is counteracted in communion, a way of giving and sharing that requires the intimacy of brokenness.

It's happening all around us and I can almost see it: once you dare to take the broken way, stay with the broken, daily give forward even your brokenness, your broken heart is enlightened— it becomes light. Like all His light, filled with all His light.

Your heart learns a new way of being—a paradoxical abundant broken way.

It can only be learned in *koinonia*, with Christ and with His body. Communion is our course to abundance. Communion is the way Jesus ultimately came to show us, because ultimately, the givenness of communion is the essence of really living. *Koinonia* is always, always the miracle and there is no other way to enter abundance.

Hope and I are about out of breath, but filled, wheat humming in the rush of our running, hearts pounding alive in our ears. I was born in the middle of a wheat harvest and all this gold will be harvested tomorrow and its kernels will run through our open hands. There isn't one stalk in this field that's afraid to be cut.

It's the broken hearts that find the haunting loveliness of a new beat—it's the broken hearts that live a song that echoes God's.

Beat, beloved heart, beat on in the world.
You will be broken and you will be loved.
You don't ever have to be afraid.

The way keeps opening up before us.
And we'll let it come.

How Did I Live Given Today?

#betheGIFT

When you *sacrifice* for what you love, you *gain* more of what you *love.*

How Did I Live Given Today?

#betheGIFT

You can give without
loving, but you cannot
love without giving.

—AMY CARMICHAEL

How Did I Live Given Today?

#betheGIFT

> Whatever is given to Christ is immediately touched with immortality.
>
> —A. W. TOZER

How Did I Live Given Today?

#betheGIFT

Love is a willingness to suffer.

How Did I Live Given Today?

#betheGIFT

Bad brokenness is broken by *good* brokenness.

How Did I Live Given Today?

#betheGIFT

> The only things we can keep are the things we freely give to God.
>
> —C. S. LEWIS

Gift Ideas

○ *1.*   Want an empty bucket list? Pour out your life. Set out a jar, bowl, or container as a life visual.

○ *2.*   Give someone the ministry of presence, and sit for just five minutes longer.

○ *3.*   *Hug* someone today who might not expect it.

○ *4.*   Wave at every truck driver you see today.

○ *5.*   Write just three lines of encouragement to someone feeling broken.

○ *6.*   Belly laugh with someone. Look for *laughter* and multiply it.

○ *7.*   Hold a door for one person today and say to them what you'd want to hear.

○ *8.*   *Connect* with one person today with whom it's been too long.

○ *9.*   Compliment someone today who it'd be easier not to.

○ *10.* Share something you've read with someone today.

○ *11.* Say as many *hellos* as you can today.

○ *12.* Forgive today. Think forgiveness. #betheGIFT. Give It Forward Today.

○ *13.* Help one person today with a job or chore that's theirs, not yours.

○ *14.* Connect—text, call, or message—someone who you've seen as very different from you.

○ *15.* Do one thing outside your *comfort zone* for someone else.

○ *16.* Choose the ministry of smiling at everyone today. It's contagious!

○ *17.* Scribble down a thank-you for your mail person. Leave it where they will find it.

○ *18.* You love as well as you're inconvenienced. Be inconvenienced in some way for someone.

○ *19.* Say *thank you* to as many people as you can today.

○ *20.* Send a Bible verse or a "praying for you" text.

○ *21.* Give away something you find hard to *give*.

○ 22. Call a parent or child and thank them for a good memory.

○ 23. Risk in some way something of yourself today for someone. Love large.

○ 24. Hand out as many *compliments* today as you can.

○ 25. Find a fight song or anthem. Send it to a friend in need of tunes and "listen" together via text, call, FaceTime, etc.

○ 26. Send a thirty-second video to someone *hurting*.

○ 27. Write one thank-you note to someone from at least ten years in your past.

○ 28. *Invite* just one person to one thing today.

○ 29. Ask "How can I help?" as many times as possible today.

○ 30. Set three alarms. *Pray* three times today for someone hurting.

○ 31. Live cruciform: *sacrifice* one thing today for someone.

○ 32. Think of three gifts each day you are thankful for—and then reach out to thank the three people who directly or indirectly make those gifts possible!

33. Mail the craziest, zaniest, wackiest gift to someone. Fun fact: Did you know you can mail an inflated beach ball?

34. Print out fifty "You are so LOVED!" cards, and hide them in the pages of books at the library, on shelves in the supermarket, or on tables in the mall food court.

35. Grab a group of friends, and *serenade* strangers on the street.

36. *Affirm* three people today for their work.

37. Leave the biggest tip you can afford, and write your server a thank-you note. You never know how it might affect their day.

38. Stand on a street corner for a set amount of time, and give compliments to everyone you see!

39. Tell as many people as you can today that you *love* their smile.

40. Give someone the *benefit* of the doubt.

41. Order a pizza for a friend who's feeling down. Have it delivered to their door. *Bonus points if you get the restaurant to shape the pepperoni into a smiley face. :)

○ 42. Let that car merge in front of you in the middle of *busy* traffic.

○ 43. Involved in a group conversation? Go out of your way to make sure each person feels included.

○ 44. Make a *donation* of any amount to a group or cause of your choosing.

○ 45. Reach out across dividing lines and say "Hi" to a friend who might be a little different from you.

○ 46. Print off at least one of the *fun* photos stuck in your phone, and mail some out to the friends who are in them!

○ 47. While out and about, compliment a parent on how well his/her child is behaving.

○ 48. Take a *photo* of anything you see that reminds you of someone, and send it their way. It's a fun way to say "Thinking of you!"

○ 49. Go through your closet and "gift" your unneeded clothing to a shelter or secondhand shop near you.

○ 50. Sweep up the *leaves* in your neighbor's yard.

○ *51.* Give someone five minutes when you don't think you have it.

○ *52.* Let someone else take that *coveted* parking space . . .

○ *53.* Practice the ministry of with-ness! Go with a friend to an event, and cheer them on with all your heart!

○ *54.* Share food in a *meaningful* way with someone today.

○ *55.* #betheGIFT when you're out shopping! Thank as many retail workers and store clerks as possible.

○ *56.* Live a *life* of thanksgiving. Thank someone older and younger than you today.

○ *57.* Spend twenty minutes with someone you love. Ask questions and just listen.

○ *58.* Hug someone. Tell them they're *needed.*

○ *59.* Send an email to a former teacher, and thank them for the impact they made on your life.

○ *60.* Text someone—just to say good morning or good night!